AF443746

k, Rai
vel car

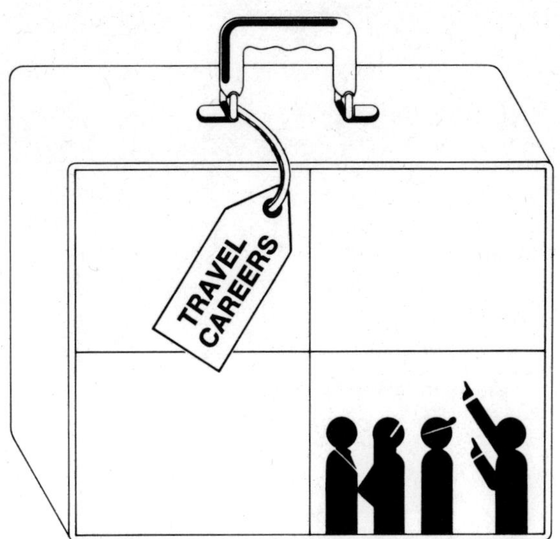
TRAVEL
CAREERS

FRANKLIN WATTS
NEW YORK | LONDON | 1976

TRAVEL CAREERS

BY RALPH H. PECK

ILLUSTRATED BY
MARK RUBIN

To my aunt
Rebecca Howard

Library of Congress Cataloging in Publication Data

Peck, Ralph H
    Travel careers.

    (A Career concise guide)
    Includes index.
    SUMMARY: Describes job opportunities in
the travel industry and the education and training
needed for them.
    1. Tourist trade — Vocational guidance — Juve-
nile literature. [1. Tourist trade — Vocational guid-
ance. 2. Vocational guidance] I. Rubin, Mark, 1946–
II. Title.
G155.5.P42   338.4′7′91023   75–43730
ISBN 0–531–01154–2

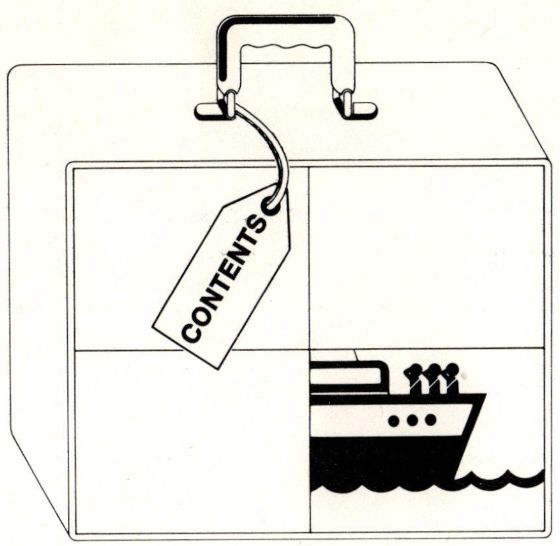
CONTENTS

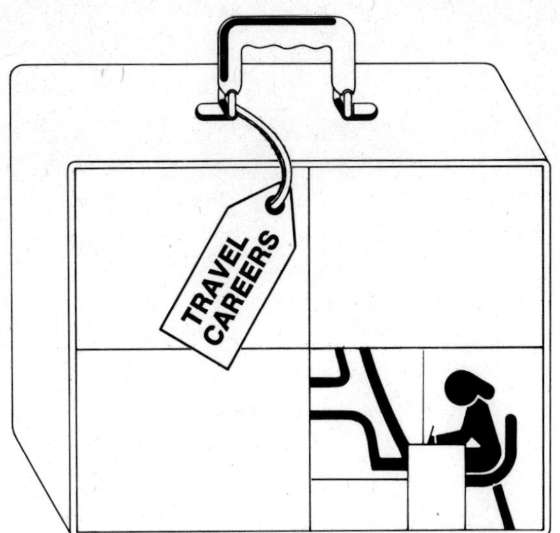
TRAVEL
CAREERS

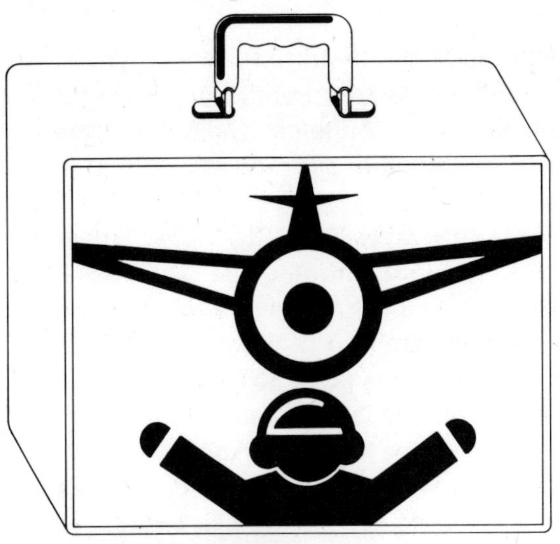

AIRLINE WORKERS

CABIN ATTENDANTS

For air travelers, the most visible airline representatives are cabin, or flight, attendants—stewardesses, stewards, pursers, and flight directors. They make in-flight announcements, demonstrate how to use oxygen masks and life jackets, serve cocktails and meals, and act as hosts and hostesses. In short, their job is to make flying comfortable.

Cabin crew work is demanding and tiring, and it requires both physical stamina and an outgoing personality. Hours can be long—many international flights last eight to ten hours. An ability to remain calm and smiling throughout each flight is important.

Jane Hanson, a stewardess on U.S. domestic routes with Trans World Airlines (TWA) for seven years, said that "on my very first vacation, to Florida, I thought that work as a cabin attendant was far beyond anything I could ever do. The girls on that flight worked so hard. And I thought that if I ever had to face so many people on an airplane I'd be too frightened to do anything." Still, Jane became a stewardess.

[1]

At ease and enthusiastic about her work after seven years, Jane handled her duties efficiently and personably on a flight from Newark, New Jersey, to Los Angeles, California. She spoke with quick humor to passengers, showing an interest in them as individuals.

Jane Hanson's day began in a New York City hotel, where she had shared a room for the night with another stewardess. (Roommating is standard practice with some airlines.) She rose at 8:15 A.M. New York time and had to be at Newark Airport by 9:30. The flight's departure was at 10:30 A.M.

After checking in at the Operations Office, Jane boarded the plane, a Boeing 707. The 707s have been workhorse aircraft for airlines since Pan American World Airways introduced jets in 1958. They were the first jets used for commercial passenger flights. Before that, propeller aircraft had been used exclusively.

Aboard the plane, Jane's first duty was to check the emergency equipment. Following that, she checked the number of prepackaged meals in the tourist-class galley and soft drinks, wines, and liquors on board to make certain there were enough for the number of passengers who would soon come on board.

When passengers began to arrive, Jane helped them locate their seats and stow their luggage. Two people, somewhat nervous, asked for aspirin; she provided it, with water. Before the flight departed, Jane counted the passengers, making sure that the count matched the list supplied to her. She demonstrated how to use oxygen masks. Then she took orders for lunch and drinks.

Before takeoff, she and the other cabin attendants took seats and remained in them until the flight had reached cruising altitude at about 25,000 feet. Then they began to serve drinks and to prepare hot meals.

During meal service on that flight, one attendant did the cooking for tourist-class passengers, another did the serving. When there are more than eighty passengers in the tourist section, two attendants serve meals. Jane had a smaller load, and she did the serving alone. In the smaller first-class section, two attendants usually handle the more elaborate cooking and tray arrangements, and both serve drinks and meals. Once passengers have finished eating and trays have been removed, stewards and stewardesses may relax near the galley. They remain alert to passenger requests, however. That may include serving drinks, providing pillows and blankets, helping people fasten seat belts if weather gets bumpy, or providing assistance with making arrangements for connecting flights. When movies are shown on a flight, attendants generally have less to do. They also have less to do at night when most passengers sleep.

Jane Hanson is a senior stewardess. It usually takes a stewardess four or five years to reach the senior level. However, the length of time required to reach the senior level does vary at different airlines. At some companies, employees must apply for senior positions according to union rules. Other airlines may promote cabin attendants to senior levels to fill openings when other senior people leave the company.

Jane's senior status has several rewards: she flies only four times a month, each trip lasting three days. She does not have to work on Fridays, on weekends, or on Mondays during the day. A senior level also means a higher salary.

This is how Jane described her work schedule: "On Monday night, I left Los Angeles for Boston, where we arrived on Tuesday morning. After spending the night at a hotel in Boston, I flew to St. Louis on Wednesday morning and worked back east aboard another flight from St. Louis to New York City that afternoon. We arrived in New York at 6:30 P.M. on Wednesday, spent the night, and departed for Los Angeles from Newark (Thursday morning)." That's four flights, not counting stops en route. Between Monday and Thursday nights, Jane Hanson flew 10,000 miles. She greeted and served more than five hundred passengers.

Different airlines have different vacation policies. Jane gets twenty-three vacation days. If she wishes, she can split her vacation into three separate periods, taking a week or more at different times of the year. On vacations, Jane has traveled in Greece, Israel, Spain, and France, and she's taken several trips within the United States.

On Fridays and Mondays, Jane attends a college, where she studies liberal arts subjects and speech therapy. "Lots of cabin attendants have taken law degrees and master's degrees in their free time," she revealed.

Before applying for work as a cabin attendant, Jane Hanson had been in nursing school for two years. Nursing wasn't the career she wanted, she decided. "My nursing school background helped, I think, but it wasn't required for employment as a stewardess," she said. "At that time, the airline looked for easygoing personalities, attractive and well-groomed people. Applicants also had to be mature enough to live away from home. Applicants with at least two years of college were preferred at that time, but several people with only a high school diploma were hired."

Before she was assigned as a flight stewardess, Jane spent five weeks at TWA's Flight Training School in a suburb of Kansas City, Missouri.

**Cabin
Attendant
Requirements**

Requirements at different airlines for cabin attendants are basically the same. For specifics considered important by interviewers, Pan American World Airways' former Management Recruitment Director and Flight Service Personnel Supervisor Sally Cutler provided insights. Because Pan American flies only on international routes, it has one distinctive "must" not required by domestic airlines. "All cabin attendants must have a fair proficiency in at least one foreign language as well as fluency in English."

Minimum age at Pan American for flight attendants is twenty. A high school diploma is sufficient, but nowadays most cabin attendants—at Pan Am and elsewhere—have attended college for two years or more. Many also traveled abroad (before employment), where they acquired foreign language proficiency.

At this writing, the minimum height at Pan American is 5'2".

Sally Cutler said that maximum height has been 6′5″ for stewards, although that may change. (People shorter than 5′2″ would have difficulty trying to reach storage compartments.) Weight should be in proportion to the individual's height.

Airlines with flights to foreign countries require stewards and stewardesses to understand and speak at least one foreign language.

One more point about languages: if an employee has only "fair fluency" in a foreign tongue—meaning ability to understand simple questions and answers, and to read the foreign language in-flight announcements—further study is required; such employees must "raise the fluency degree to good or excellent within six months." After a six-month probation period, tests are given to new employees to determine whether they've improved satisfactorily. The airline maintains language laboratories at bases, with tapes and playback equipment for use by in-flight personnel. Generally, considerable language improvement is possible within six months. Cabin attendants have ample opportunities between flights to practice their languages at foreign destinations.

To qualify at American-owned international airlines as a flight attendant, American citizenship is not an absolute necessity. However, foreign applicants must have a permanent U.S. immigration visa; they also must maintain a United States resident status and be able to fly to *all* Pan Am destinations. (Some foreign nationals are forbidden entry to certain countries, which automatically would disqualify them for in-flight employment.) Fluency in a foreign language is one reason American-owned international airlines hire foreign-born workers.

Although it formerly was standard practice at airlines to hire only single women as cabin attendants, this restriction has been lifted. Many are married, some are mothers, and men, both single and married, are being hired. When some airlines hired only women cabin attendants, it was judged as discriminatory against men. Now both sexes are hired and opportunities are equal. Maternity leaves and other liberating benefits have been introduced.

AIRLINE TICKET OFFICE AGENT

The Pan American World Airways ticket office in Hartford, Connecticut, is an off-line office in a city where the carrier has no flights. The staff is comparatively small. Therefore, the work is more demanding than at larger offices where each individual may have specialized duties. The employees work with travel agents and commercial accounts, serve customers who stop at the office, and answer telephone queries about schedules, fares, and tours.

Horace "Pete" Morison, Jr., has been a senior ticket office agent in Hartford for several years. Before he was employed by Pan Am in New York (where he worked for four years until his transfer to Hartford at his request), he was graduated from Harvard University with a bachelor's degree in government. He had also been in the army as a first lieutenant and later worked in Austria for the U.S. Displaced Persons Commission. He is fluent in German and French.

Said Pete: "I chose to go with Pan Am because I like people, and because I wanted to be associated with an international airline. I felt I could offer enthusiasm for foreign destinations because of my lifelong travel background and my work in Europe. I've always had a liking for historic places, for foreign customs and affairs." As a child, he had traveled abroad widely with his family.

Pete Morison described his work schedule. "When I arrive at the office, I first set up the ticket counter for the day. That means ensuring that the office machines and telephones are in working order, that there are enough travel folders in the racks. Then I make out tourist cards. (They're information forms stating why travelers will be in certain Latin American countries, how long they plan to stay, their nationality, their home address, and their ages. Some must be written in Spanish.) In Hartford, we often do this for travel agents.

"Throughout the day, I answer telephone calls. We get questions about fares and immigration, ticketing, clearing wait lists on particular flights, and health immunization. Travel agents request supplies of booklets, ticket validation stickers, and similar materials," Pete said.

"We also reissue tickets." Whenever a passenger requires a change of route, or in the number of days spent at different places, new tickets must be issued. On world tours, fifty or more tickets may have to be changed. A reissue also requires cancellation of existing reservations at hotels and on all flights. Such changes often mean different hours of arrival and departure, as well as use of different airlines, trains, buses, or ships. It's a complicated procedure.

"Considerable military business also comes through Hartford —servicemen and their families returning to the States or going overseas. Government transportation requests also come into our office.

"Besides these duties, we deal with the general public at the ticket counter. Most of our traffic is to Jamaica, to Latin and Central America, Barbados, Guyana, Europe, and generally to the Caribbean, in that order."

Pete Morison has some accounting duties, too. "We get a lot of prepaid tickets for people coming from abroad to visit relatives here." (A prepaid ticket, in this case, would be a ticket paid for in the United States, to be used by someone visiting here from another country.)

As a senior employee at Pan American, Pete gets five weeks vacation. He's allowed two free vacation tickets annually, plus unlimited travel at a ten- to twenty-dollar service charge. His wife and children (the children until they're of age) are allowed the same travel benefits. Pete has traveled in the Middle East, New Zealand, Hawaii, the Caribbean, South America, and often to Europe. His wife and children have often vacationed at exotic destinations with him.

Applying for a
Ticket Office or
Reservations Job

Personnel offices at airlines will supply you with application forms. If your background indicates that you're suitable for a reservations job, you will be given a personal interview.

A good knowledge of geography, an ability to cope with detailed work, and an outgoing personality are important. Since fares and taxes must be figured, mathematical facility also is required.

For those who deal directly with the public at ticket offices and check-in counters, a neat, clean-cut appearance takes precedence. Anyone who arrives at a personnel office with sloppy clothing, unkempt hair, and undisciplined manners should not expect to be hired. Most counter personnel wear uniforms. The tradition of military or naval spit-and-polish prevails, for that's the image projected by airline people. This very particular "look" sets a theme—correctness, efficiency, training, a desire to give good service—that's as important to airlines as expensive advertising and promotion.

If you're unwilling to conform to these specifics, you will waste your time—and the time devoted to you by those who process applications and conduct interviews—in applying for a job in this category.

Training

Most airlines conduct training classes for reservations and ticket office personnel. Generally they last from a month to six weeks, and new employees are paid while they attend classes. They learn geography, routes, destination codes (HKG for Hong Kong, BOS for Boston, and so forth), airline codes, reference manual usage, teletype message techniques, how to use computers, fares, and other subjects necessary for their work.

If you're hired for telephone reservations, you may be taught telephone techniques. (When you smile while you're talking on the telephone, for instance, the person you're talking with receives an image of a smiling, pleasant personality. Try it; it really works.) Those chosen for work at counters are also instructed in ways to project a likable, helpful personality.

Recently sales approaches have been stressed. There are "right" and "wrong" methods, and airlines in the highly competitive travel-selling arena are in business to make money. Since reservations people usually are the first contacts between customers and airlines, selling techniques are explained and practiced.

In most classes, students play "roles" with classmates to prepare for actual work circumstances. One pretends to be a customer; another, the reservations or ticket agent. Instructors lead students through procedures to be followed, ways to clinch a sale, every step necessary through completed bookings and ticketing.

TELEPHONE RESERVATIONS AGENT

An ability "to sell travel and transportation" is a requirement for reservations agents at Trans World Airlines. Reservations agents have sales quotas, which means that they must book a certain amount of business. In order to ensure that they're meeting quotas, their selling performances are reviewed regularly. The salesperson who regularly does not meet the quota may be given a chance to switch to another job or may be fired.

To sell travel or any other product, the individual in the job must be aggressive. This doesn't mean being pushy in a derogatory sense; aggressiveness can be a positive quality. Aggressiveness suggests that reservations agents must take the lead. They should attempt to complete a business transaction, to steer a telephone caller into a firm booking.

An example: a caller wants to know about flights on a certain date, and the costs. An aggressive reservations agent would check the flights and add that "I can reserve seats for you on that flight now."

Should a caller be reluctant to make a firm reservation, he or she might be convinced by the reservations agent that it's advisable because that flight is already booked heavily. "You may be unable to travel on that date without an advance reservation." To complete the booking the agent might suggest that "you always can cancel and rebook a flight with us on a later date, if necessary. But a reservation now will protect you for the time being."

This aggressive approach is reconstructed from several telephone calls I monitored at TWA's Reservations Center in New York. Several firm bookings resulted. The reason for this approach is this: when a prospective passenger already holds a reservation with TWA, chances are that the person will keep it. Or if the passenger should make a change, he or she most likely will rebook with TWA. Reservations agents' telephones are monitored by supervisors to check that they're handling their jobs effectively. Agents also can signal that they wish aid from supervisors through the monitor board.

Anne Joyce has been a reservations agent at TWA in New York for eight and a half years. She works from 12:30 P.M. until 5 P.M. six days in a row. During mornings, she attends college. She's majoring in accounting.

"Computers we use now are newer models, more modern than the ones we had when I first started with TWA," Anne said. On her six-day work schedule, she has no permanent days off, not every Wednesday or every Saturday. "On this work cycle, I occasionally get two days off together, sometimes four days free. Whenever I have four days off, I usually take a trip."

When she enters the office, Anne first checks the mailbox. Then she jots down how many calls have been taken at her desk position by the time she arrived at work. At 5:30, before she leaves, she enters the new number, which shows exactly how many calls she's taken during her work shift.

Anne handles both domestic and international travel. "The most typical calls I get are from secretaries checking for their bosses. They usually want to know when a particular flight departs for Chicago or to some other large city."

Computers supply Anne with most of the information she needs, flashing (on a desk-size television screen) excursion fares, schedules, whether or not flights are sold out. If fares are complicated—or if an itinerary requires special fare computations—Anne requests the information from rate specialists.

While I sat with Anne at her desk, she received a call from a man with a foreign accent. "What flight do you have on Saturday?" he asked.

"To where?" Anne replied.

The man told her that he expected a friend to arrive in New York from Portugal at 4:10 P.M. that day. Anne checked flight arrivals from Portugal and determined that TWA had no flight arriving from Lisbon at that time. Another airline was scheduled to arrive at that time, however, and she gave the man the telephone number to call for information. He thanked her for her helpfulness.

Later, a woman whose husband was on assignment with a film company in Florence, Italy, wanted to know about flights there. Anne advised her that there were no services by air into Florence on the date requested. TWA could accommodate the woman and her child to Rome or to Milan, she said, where train connections could be made to Florence. "Since no other airline goes into Florence at this time of year, you may as well fly TWA. Right?" The woman made a reservation for two.

When she started working at TWA, Anne had attended college for one and a half years. She had also spent a summer in Europe. A friend told her that the airline was interviewing for reservations people. She applied and was hired. She'd previously worked part time at Macy's department store in sales, and the TWA personnel department thought that was good experience working with people.

Originally, Anne thought she wanted to be an English teacher. Now accounting appeals to her more. "I like math, figures, and accounting is a field that pays well. I can apply accounting at TWA, and I don't have to remain in New York to do that. I want to stay with the airline, and accounting is ideal for me from a business standpoint. Accounting opens several management opportunities, and a big airline has diversified possibilities. It's not as limited as a small company. Salaries are competitive, too, or better."

As a part-time employee, Anne is ineligible for retirement or investment plans open to full-time employees. However, she may belong to the credit union, and she enjoys medical, dental, life insurance, and travel benefits.

FOREIGN AIRLINE—
PRESS
RELATIONS

Public relations and *press relations* are interchangeable phrases. Some airlines use one title, some another.

In this category you'll find people who work alone or with others to promote an air carrier's full services, destinations, routes, and tours. There are also people with special assignments. Sports program supervisors, for example. Or fashion coordinators, who may lecture on what to wear when traveling and give advice to women travelers. Or cargo experts working with elements totally different from passenger services, although cargo also includes heavy traffic in corpses.

Public relations staffs establish liaison between their companies and the media—magazine and newspaper editors, television and radio outlets. They may also take charge of employee relations through company magazines. Some may work directly with the public, showing films and lecturing. Others may write speeches for busy company executives. Whatever their particular role may be, they're expected to help build the best possible public acceptance for their airline. The professional public relations representative aids advertising by getting free editorial coverage and mentions by columnists as often as possible, thereby keeping the company image before the public.

The primary requirement for a professional public relations representative is an ability to write. Because the "news peg" (or story slant that makes the difference between getting material in print and having it thrown in a waste basket) is extremely important, job interviewers look for a background in journalism.

Years ago public relations people had reputations similar to those of circus barkers. They'd do anything to get people in to see the show, or to buy a product. That's changed. Now most public relations people are professional, marketing experts and good writers. They know how to deal with other writers and editors, and their work is respected. But they've kept one trait of the old-time circus barker—they're friendly and likable.

Applicants for airline public relations spots are expected to have experience in the travel industry. Since working as a reporter or editor for travel industry trade publications combines writing and an extensive background in travel and transportation, many people enter public relations departments directly from trade journals. It's a logical career move. Trade reporters establish wide associations throughout the travel industry. Because of this, their work is known, and they're most likely to be approached when an airline has a public relations job to fill. The trade writers also have had an opportunity to build working relationships with other media representatives, who are important to effective publicity.

Lucille Hoshabjian is press relations manager for North and Central America at Lufthansa German Airlines. She works in New York, where her responsibilities have expanded steadily since she joined the airline. She coordinates activities for six regional public relations managers.

One unique aspect of Lucille's work is that she handles a variety of public relations assignments: financial and cargo public relations as well as passenger services promotion. She works with writers and editors in all media, writes speeches, authors articles for the company's bimonthly magazine (*Jet Tales*), and sets up familiarization and inaugural tours for press representatives.

Lucille Hoshabjian is a professional. She knows where failures can occur in placing editorial material, and she's thorough when she has something special to promote. As an example: I recently covered a Lufthansa press reception for a magazine. Lucille met and spoke with every writer present, ensuring that each received a press kit outlining the details and including speeches made by Lufthansa officials. Later she telephoned an editor at the magazine I represented to ask if he might want additional pictures or information to go with my story. (At big magazines, editors don't always know who has covered a particular story.) Lucille's call alerted the editor that he could expect my article, and also that she was anxious to get good placement on the news pages. She had left nothing to chance. Her follow-through paid dividends. The story landed on the first page. And that's good public relations.

"Most of what I do in this job is anonymous," Lucille Hoshabjian asserted. "It's not a place for the individual who likes to see his by-line on stories." She further observed that "traditionally public relations at foreign airlines has been open to women." That hadn't been generally true at American air carriers until recently, she believes, but it's improving.

She explained that she was hired at Lufthansa because the airline wanted an American with press-writing experience who spoke German. She's fluent in German and also speaks Italian, French, Spanish, and Armenian.

"I feel secure in public relations," Lucille declared, "because, frankly, I feel that I'm a better news writer than a creative writer, which suits the needs of this job. Free-lance writing requires much more creativity, a more contemplative, imaginative style, and I'm not at ease with it. I belong in news, and that's what this work is all about, with a few million other demands."

From Upper Darby, Pennsylvania, Lucille Hoshabjian earned her bachelor of arts degree in journalism at Temple University, where she had a scholarship. She'd worked on the school newspaper in high school and on her college yearbook. Immediately after college, she worked in West Berlin (in a job with a top-secret classification) for two years for the United States government. During that time she traveled widely throughout Europe and studied German.

After returning to the United States, she found it difficult to translate her government-job experience into work that interested her. But finally she was able to find a temporary job with *Esquire* magazine. From there she joined a travel industry trade publication called *Travel Europe.* While working there, she also co-authored a 300-page book, *Europe Up-to-Date.* Her work with a travel trade publication opened opportunities to do free-lance writing, and she left for Europe again, where she filed articles from Spain and Italy.

Returning to the United States again, she joined the public relations staff for the Commonwealth of Puerto Rico in 1967. In 1968 her contract was terminated. That's when she was hired at Lufthansa. Her editorial/writing experience, her travels, her wide contacts within the travel industry, and her languages were assets.

Benefits

Public relations representatives for airlines have travel benefits. In some cases that means sizable discounts for vacation travel; sometimes it's free. Representatives also may go as supervisors on travel agent and journalists' familiarization trips. Supervising such trips is hard work. The problems involved are more than simply taking a trip with a group.

A tour leader must see that baggage is delivered properly and is responsible for exchanging tickets, if necessary. The leader must be sure that everyone in the group is ready to depart on time for each leg of the trip. The leader is the one who must cope with complaints, make provisions if someone gets sick, and generally serve as the host.

Not everyone can take charge of a traveling group effectively. It calls for diplomacy and a capacity to be friendly with everyone while asserting the authority required from a group leader. When a tour leader is unable to guide a group efficiently, the inability reflects poorly on the company represented. And that's bad public relations.

Other Possibilities

Foreign language proficiency is unimportant if you're interested in a public relations job with a domestic American air carrier. There are plentiful opportunities nationally and regionally. Interviewers look for a journalism background and an easygoing personality.

Airline Addresses

Following is a selected list of airlines, where you may write for further information. Many excellent airlines are not included in this list. To be complete would take several more pages.

Dun and Bradstreet Directories (which you may find in most libraries) have complete lists of transportation companies. Another useful reference is *Standard and Poor's Register of Corporations, Directors and Executives.*

Air France
1350 Avenue of the Americas
New York, New York 10019

American Airlines
633 Third Avenue
New York, New York 10017

Allegheny Airlines
National Airport
Washington, D.C. 20001

Braniff International
P.O. Box 35001
Dallas, Texas 75235

Continental Air Lines
Los Angeles International
   Airport
Los Angeles, California 90009

Delta Air Lines
Hartsfield Atlanta International
   Airport
Atlanta, Georgia 30320

Eastern Air Lines
10 Rockefeller Plaza
New York, New York 10020

El Al Israel Airlines
850 Third Avenue
New York, New York 10022

Hughes Airwest
San Francisco International
   Airport
San Francisco,
   California 94128

Irish International Airlines
564 Fifth Avenue
New York, New York 10036

Japan Airlines
655 Fifth Avenue
New York, New York 10022

Lufthansa German Airlines
1640 Hempstead Turnpike
East Meadow,
   New York 11554

National Airlines
P.O. Box 2055,
   Airport Mail Facility
Miami, Florida 33159

Northwest Orient Airlines
Minneapolis/St. Paul
   International Airport
St. Paul, Minnesota 55111

Pan American World Airways
Pan Am Building
New York, New York 10017

Scandinavian
   Airlines System
138–02 Queens Boulevard
Jamaica, New York 11435

TAP–Portuguese Airways
601 Fifth Avenue
New York, New York 10017

TWA
605 Third Avenue
New York, New York 10016

United Air Lines
P.O. Box 66100
Chicago, Illinois 60666

Western Air Lines
P.O. Box 92005
   World Way Postal Center
Los Angeles,
   California 90009

TRAVEL
AGENT

In small cities and towns where transportation companies have no offices, travel agents are the only sales representatives for tours, cruises, railroad, airline, and bus tickets. Still, travel agencies also proliferate in large cities where frequent travelers have become accustomed to their services.

Agency incomes are based on commissions paid by transportation companies. Most travel agencies charge no extra fees for their services.

Tom Patten became a travel agent five years ago. After graduation from college with a liberal arts degree and traveling for three months in Europe, he became interested in working in the travel field. He discovered while in Europe that he enjoyed exploring foreign places, learning about historical and architectural legacies, and speaking foreign languages. To nourish these interests, he applied for work as an airline reservations agent. He was hired by a foreign airline with offices in Chicago, where he worked for two years.

At the airline, Tom learned about routes, ticketing, tour packages, air/sea plans (travel by plane and ship), rental cars, hotel bookings, excursion and family fares. He was immersed in detailed planning, selling, and booking passenger seats and accommodations throughout the world. When he was offered a job in a small travel agency, he accepted. It was a lateral move, from one sales position into another. But although Tom's airline and agency work are related, the differences were obvious from his first day with the agency.

Travel agents become involved in all types of travel. They often sell travel plans to which airline reservations people have little exposure. Cruises and bus tours are examples. The intricacies are different, too. Travel agents may be expected to order tickets to the La Scala Opera in Milan, or to arrange for a guide, car, and chauffeur to take someone to an isolated shrine in southern France. In airline reservations such requests are made, but reservations agents are less likely to handle them regularly. In a sense, Tom Patten is confronted by a more complex travel world since he became a travel agent.

There are other differences. Automated equipment at airlines flashes information on closed-circuit television. Few small agencies can afford sophisticated data processing, teletype machines, and other equipment available at airlines. Agency work also requires different disciplines. The busy agent calculates fares and taxes. He writes tickets by hand that are produced mechanically at some airlines.

On the day we met, Tom Patten booked a honeymoon couple for a week in Bermuda; the couple began traveling in Atlanta, stopped in New York, then went on to Hamilton, Bermuda. On their return, they went directly to Chicago.

That day Tom also wrote and posted letters for accommodations at small hotels in Paris and Buenos Aires. He quoted costs for a world cruise and booked people on flights to Miami and Las Vegas. He had to plan a complicated trip through the Far East, with train transportation in Malaysia and a fishing-boat charter in Penang.

People expect their travel agents to know the good and bad points about hotels and ships. They want advice about taxi fares as compared to airport bus fares in out-of-the-way places. Travel agents are asked about tipping, about climate and what to wear, about documentation and inoculations requirements, about restaurants, art galleries, and guide services.

While I was with him, Tom Patten talked with a widely traveled woman who was going on safari in East Africa. "What's a good Chinese restaurant in Nairobi?" she asked. Without hesitating, he recommended the Bamboo Shoot Restaurant. But Tom was curious. "Why do you want a Chinese restaurant in Nairobi?"

"Because Chinese food is dependable," the woman said. "I always worry about food in foreign countries."

That's where Tom Patten's travel experience was invaluable. He explained that Nairobi, Kenya, is a cosmopolitan, modern city, that the restaurants there serve superb food prepared as well as or better than in many other great cities. His counsel was that the woman had no need to worry about food in Nairobi, nor even in outlying game lodges in Kenya.

Tom traveled throughout the world to learn these things while he was an airline employee. He has continued to travel as a travel agent, inspecting accommodations, keeping abreast of changes in services.

Good travel agents constantly recheck facilities during their travels, for the more they know about every destination and the services found there, the better they may serve and advise their clients. People depend on their travel agents.

Free familiarization tours are offered regularly to travel agents. On properly organized tours, they have an opportunity to explore tourist sites, to inspect hotels and restaurants, and to evaluate vacation areas. In addition to free familiarization travel, agents are also allowed substantial discounts for air and sea travel, at hotels, and on tour buses.

Job Requirements

Lee Kleeman opened her own small travel agency in New York City five years ago. She had worked for another travel agency for three years before she went into business on her own. "I could never have survived in this business without experience," she declared. Lee works hard, six days a week, running her agency with three employees, two of whom work part time.

In hiring for Lee Kleeman World Travel, Ltd., Lee believes that the years spent in school or college are less important than an airline ticketing background, an ability to handle detailed work, and wide travel experience. "You certainly can't give advice about places if you haven't been there," she said.

"Anyone who wants to be a travel agent really has to enjoy travel," Lee stated. "I look for people with a nice telephone personality, those who like people and can work with them in planning an extensive vacation or a quick business trip."

The question about how much formal education a job applicant should have for work at a travel agency varies with the employer. In New York City, for example, where there's tremendous competition for every job opening, employers can be choosy. They can demand college education, refined skills, and two or three years experience, and they can get it. Lee Kleeman's remarks were made with the New York City labor market in view, where well-qualified people are available.

Furthermore, wide international travel implies a good education, most often some college, and perhaps facility in foreign languages. People who travel widely also tend to develop independent, self-starting personalities. They require less supervision. Keeping in mind that airline reservations experience is sought for those who go into travel agency work, it follows that travel agents will have the background required by airlines. Often, that means at least two years of college.

Although it's less common in large cities than in smaller communities, travel agency employees sometimes work up to sales and consultant jobs from secretarial and clerical positions. This occurs most often in areas where the daily work load is comparatively relaxed, the pace less demanding. Under such circumstances, there's time to acquire skills on the job. It takes about six months to train a travel agent. Since many small agencies are family-owned, some owners' relatives and wives work in the office; they're mostly trained on the job.

[21]

Training Opportunities

After they've worked at an agency for six months or longer, travel agency employees may attend classes conducted by airlines. Some sessions are held in large cities, and they usually last for a day or two, covering only one or two important subjects. Once or twice a year, some airlines also offer week-long courses; for those, air transportation and hotel accommodations are provided at minimal cost.

Familiarization trips (sometimes free, and by invitation), domestic and international travel at discounted prices, and special low hotel rates are among the benefits enjoyed by travel agents. They also are invited to evening receptions and to sales presentations aboard ships and at big hotels. These advantages invest travel agency work with a life-style that appeals to many people.

Further Information

Thousands of travel agency addresses and telephone numbers are listed in telephone directory "Yellow Pages" throughout the United States. Usually, travel agents near where you live can answer any questions you may have.

TOUR OPERATOR

Tour operators sell "packaged tours" to the public through travel agencies and airlines, and sometimes directly through their retail offices. A tour plan—including air, ship, bus, rail, or auto transportation, hotel accommodations, baggage transfers, meals, everything the traveler requires—is sold for a specific price. The tour operator assembles the package, prices it for reasonable profit, and lists it as an offering. Brochures usually describe what is included.

If you want a two-week tour to Germany, through the Middle East, or to some U.S. national parks, a travel agent may advise you that a special plan is available. Usually costs for packaged plans are lower than individually arranged travel (custom plans) because tour operators depend on volume sales (large groups) for their profits. The more people who buy their packaged tours, the more money they make. Tour operation profits are based on discounts arranged with carriers, hotels, and other elements in the packages.

Laurence M. Pack is an executive with Europacar, a tour packaging company. While he was in college, Laurence worked with the company part time. He began a full-time career in 1967 and completed his last two years of college by attending classes at night. He became an assistant vice-president at Europacar in January 1975.

Larry Pack decided that he was "fascinated by the travel business" when he was a part-time employee. He had majored in mathematics at the College of the City of New York (CCNY) but switched to economics because he decided it was "more applicable to travel operations." He was graduated with a B.S. in economics.

Starting with general clerical duties—answering telephones, typing forms, keeping records—Larry worked from the ground up at Europacar. "I liked the work because it wasn't routine," he revealed. "It involves a lot of personal contact—handling complaints, working at trade shows, taking charge of travel agent familiarization trips, that sort of thing.

"Nobody stands over you saying, 'Do this, do that . . .' in this work. There's a lot of self-motivation. I've become more and more involved in day-to-day management decisions and how the company makes a profit. That requires knowing the foreign monetary exchange rates, so I make a daily currency check. [The Swiss franc goes up and down in value when the German mark changes in value, for example.] We have to figure prices months in advance, which makes our 'costing' crucial to profitable margins. Changes have to be anticipated. We began to set our tour rates for next year in March this year, and the amount we charge for each hotel room, for rental cars, and other things included in our programs is affected by the economy here and abroad—just as it is in the stock market."

Because the markup on each element within a packaged tour means the difference between profit and possible heavy losses, Larry Pack's daily concern is tied intimately to how currency fluctuations and foreign economies affect the company's profits. "I wrote a computer program to cost FITs (Foreign Independent Tours), groups, etc." Larry said. "We also were able to work out foreign currency exchange settlements on a monthly basis. You'd be surprised how much we save in postage alone."

In addition to costing tours, Larry negotiates commissions for travel sales outlets. He serves as a troubleshooter on International Air Transport Association (IATA) technicalities, supervises billing, and is in charge of some personnel. He often interviews prospective employees.

Larry likes his work. "There's a great future in the travel industry," he believes. "The business potential is being tapped with much more sophistication these days, but there's still plenty that can be done. If you offer a good product and market it properly, you're way ahead in the business. That's why I like working at Europacar."

Job Requirements

At Europacar, Maureen Cortell—the boss' daughter—has several executive duties. Her brother Ray is also an officer in the family-run company.

Maureen does much of the hiring for the company. She said that "we've always had a policy of hiring summer personnel, young people on vacation from school, when our business is heaviest. We've never advertised for help because most people who come with us have been recommended by friends working here, or by former employees."

Maureen Cortell is responsible for the duties of about forty employees. In hiring new people, she looks for organizational ability, detailed work habits (correct addition, spelling names properly, getting all the needed information), and a friendly telephone personality. "I don't stress education because it really doesn't apply if the person has the other qualities I've mentioned. If a person we like has the qualities we want and has no experience in travel, that experience can be learned at the ASTA Travel School," and we would pay for the training. (ASTA, the American Society of Travel Agents, offers courses in travel agency and tour operation techniques.)

Most employees work on tour coordination, which means they take charge of particular programs. Responsibilities include sending invoices for each passenger booked to travel agents, issuing vouchers for hotel rooms, automobile rentals, meals, and other items included in packages. Coordinators also handle sales, calling on agencies, and generally promoting their packages.

Addresses

Major tour operators throughout the United States are listed every year in the Travel Industry Personnel Directory, published by *Travel Agent* magazine, 2 West Forty-sixth Street, New York, New York 10036. Included are the companies' officers. Also included are foreign tourist offices, airlines, shiplines, railroads, and state travel bureaus.

If your school or local library does not have a copy of the directory, you might suggest to the librarian that it would be useful.

HOTEL MANAGEMENT

RESIDENT MANAGER

A resident manager is responsible for a hotel's smooth business operation from day to day. The term *resident manager* comes from the time when certain staff supervisors lived in hotels and were on call anytime day and night. Nowadays, few managers actually live in hotels, except in isolated hotels, where there may be no other acceptable housing.

The resident manager establishes housekeeping standards and ensures that they're followed. He (or she) understands restaurant and front desk accounting procedures and controls, and he keeps careful watch on daily receipts and expenditures. Because he's concerned with a steady, money-making occupancy rate, he also authorizes advertising and promotional efforts to attract guests.

Jim A. Raine is the resident manager at the Four Queens Hotel in Las Vegas, Nevada. In Las Vegas—a desert resort devoted almost entirely to gambling, entertainment, and sports activities—the hotel also has a casino as an important source of income. The hotel was opened in 1965. It has 320 rooms.

The Hyatt Hotel chain bought the Four Queens recently from its original owners.

On the day we discussed his work, Jim Raine got up at 6:30 A.M. He arrived at the hotel at 7:30. As soon as he arrived, he checked to see how many guests were registered. Then he toured the entire hotel and casino, checking cleanliness and keeping notes on every aspect where he thought improvements were necessary. After that, he met with porters and housekeepers. He made suggestions and helped to solve problems that required management decisions. Each day Jim files a report with Hyatt headquarters outlining his views about changes that he believes should be made in services and facilities, and in the work assignments for the 175 employees under his direction.

Jim Raine has been in management for more than two years with the Hyatt Hotels Corporation. Before he moved to Las Vegas, he worked at a Hyatt hotel outside Palm Springs, California.

After completing high school and one and a half years in a junior college, Jim Raine began his hotel career in 1961 with the Hotel Corporation of America. His first assignment was in Anaheim, California, where Disneyland is located. He worked in the housekeeping department, as a bellhop, as a front desk clerk, and as a night auditor in the accounting department. He then moved into the food and beverage department, where he remained for one and a half years; his highest position was as assistant food and beverage manager.

At that stage in his career, Jim decided that he'd reached a plateau with little chance for advancement for several years. Deciding that sales would offer greater financial rewards, he left his hotel job to work for a food sales company. But he missed hotel work. And he returned to the field with the Hyatt chain after a year and a half in sales.

"I'd first gone into hotel work because I liked the business," Jim said. "There's a daily challenge, not the same old routine. I really missed the excitement in hotels when I was in sales, but I realized that sales experience would help me to upgrade myself for a higher job with a hotel company."

Jim Raine had assessed his situation correctly. Hyatt hired him as assistant general manager at their Disneyland Hyatt House in Anaheim. After one year, he was transferred as general manager to the Hyatt Thunderbird Hotel outside Palm Springs, California, where he remained for another year. When Hyatt acquired the Four Queens Hotel, Jim moved there as resident manager.

HOTEL FOOD AND BEVERAGE MANAGEMENT— INTERNATIONAL

At Hilton International—hotels owned by TWA since 1967, and totally separate from U.S. domestic Hilton Hotel operations— more than 22,000 employees come from fifty-two nations. It's believed that the company employs more nationalities than any other nongovernment organization in the world. Because Hilton International operates sixty-nine hotels in forty-one countries and sixty-two cities, it's not surprising that few employees are American-born. This is especially true in food and beverage management.

The food and beverage operations director at Hilton International's Queen Elizabeth Hotel in Montreal, Canada, is Robert P. Frigiere, a Frenchman. Monsieur Frigiere was born in Lyon, France, and emigrated to Canada in 1961. His hotel career derives from an early desire to travel and to live in a foreign country, he says. He wanted to avoid the 9 A.M. to 5 P.M. business routine, to learn foreign languages, and to work with food and people. His first step was to attend the Ecole Hotelière (Hotel School) in Nice, the resort on the French Riviera.

After completing courses at the hotel school, Robert Frigiere was an apprentice in three French hotels. He served his required military service in France, too, before moving to Canada. He had a letter of introduction to the management at the Queen Elizabeth Hotel, where he passed his interview successfully. He began his service there as a waiter. During the eight years before he assumed his current duties, he was a dining room captain, headwaiter, maître d', and assistant manager. He served as an assistant manager for four years before being promoted to his present responsibilities.

**International
Hotel Chain
Requirements**

Most international hotels have similar requirements for food and beverage employees. Hilton International's personnel director in New York, Gary Cole, said that "our food and beverage people have come into the job through many channels. Our thinking is that before they move into assistant food and beverage jobs, they must have kitchen experience, training in food preparation. They must actually operate a dining room or a coffee shop. And they must have thorough training in food and beverage purchasing, and be able to take full responsibility for china, silverware, glassware, sanitation, breakage, and keeping track of supplies."

Mr. Cole says that Americans usually prefer to go into hotel work that takes less time for advancement. "It usually takes at least three years to become an assistant food and beverage manager, and the apprenticeship is comparatively hard, with several menial tasks."

Garbage disposal is one of the menial duties that must be learned. To get rid of kitchen waste may be difficult in foreign countries, but it has to be done, or diseases might be spread. It's not as easy as it sounds.

For example, how is garbage collected, and by whom, and where does it go? When there is no garbage collection, something else must be worked out. Garbage can be raided by wild animals, or even by hungry people; if it's spoiled, or if it includes any poisons, it could be very dangerous. Furthermore, different laws exist in different regions throughout the world, and they must be respected.

Since every hotel has garbage, lots of it, understanding the problems that garbage can cause is important. Working out methods to dispose of garbage in the best possible way is a food and beverage department responsibility. Somebody has to do the dirty work.

Most international hotel chains look for fluency in at least one foreign language, Mr. Cole declared. Training in a hotel school or practical experience in hotel work are absolute necessities.

"Depending on the individual, we sometimes accept applicants without a hotel school degree," Mr. Cole said. "Work experience in a good hotel certainly would count. So would ability to answer questions about hotel work. Degrees take less time in European schools, where students serve as apprentices to acquire practical skills, as they do in a trade."

Americans have less opportunity "to go international" than Europeans. The best way to get into foreign work with a hotel chain is to attend a good hotel school, to become fluent in at least one foreign language, and to work in good domestic hotels in the United States. For those who would like a food and beverage management career, a degree from a hotel management school may open the door to a beginning in purchasing, or as an assistant dining room or coffee shop manager.

Training

As hotel work has become more specialized, several hotel chains have established training schools for their employees. Hilton International is among them. It has a Career Development Institute in Montreal. Management choses students from among its employees to take courses that last from four to six weeks. Courses cover food and beverage management, front office management, sales management, housekeeping, and engineering—the many jobs that go into successful hotel operations.

Hotel courses are also offered at several colleges and universities. Probably the best-known American college for hotel students is Cornell University's School of Hotel Administration. Graduates from the Cornell school work in famous hotels all over the world. Recently several lesser-known colleges have introduced hotel administration courses.

Lambuth College in Jackson, Tennessee, has introduced a program based on a trade school approach. Instructors from Holiday Inns teach students how to run hotels, motels, and restaurants. Students at Lambuth also work at Holiday Inns in the school's area to get practical experience. They also attend classes for a full month at "Holiday Inn University," the company's training school in Mississippi. Liberal arts courses round out the program.

The University of Nevada (Las Vegas) also has a hotel school where students may work at Las Vegas resort hotels for credits toward their degrees. The school for chefs at the university is one of the finest in the United States.

Hotel Companies

This short list includes some of the finest hotel companies in the United States. For hotels in your area, consult the "Yellow Pages" in your telephone directory.

Americana Hotels
605 Third Avenue
New York, New York 10016

Hilton International
Waldorf Astoria Hotel
Park Avenue
New York, New York 10022

Inter-Continental Hotels
Pan Am Building
New York, New York 10017

Hilton Hotels Corporation
    (Domestic)
720 South Michigan Avenue
Chicago, Illinois 60605

Hyatt Hotels
1338 Bayshore Highway
Burlingame, California 94010

Sheraton Hotels and
    Motor Inns
Sheraton Boulevard
Boston, Massachusetts 02210

Western International Hotels
The Olympic Hotel
Fourth and Seneca Streets
Seattle, Washington 98111

Marriott Hotels
5161 River Road
Washington, D.C. 20016

BUS TOUR ESCORT

"Leave the driving to us," the television commercials for Greyhound Lines say. Many travelers do. Greyhound and Continental Trailways are the two largest American bus companies.

In addition to providing bus transportation throughout the United States, both companies have large tour operations. That means that they hire drivers and tour guides. Greyhound's manual for travel agents is called "Greyhound World Tours," to show that the company has services in areas other than in the United States. The manual calls attention to company operations in Mexico and as far away as Australia. Escorted tours have become increasingly important.

Lloyd L. Smith has been a Greyhound bus driver for eighteen years. When I met him, he was the driver/guide on a tour to three U.S. national parks—Zion, Bryce Canyon, and the North Rim of the Grand Canyon. I traveled with him for four days on a group tour, observing his work and how he approached it.

Not all bus drivers are guides—and some guides have never driven a bus—but Lloyd is expert at both. He's worked for Greyhound throughout the West. He knows his territory and points out details that give it new dimension and interest for travelers in his groups.

Outside Mesquite, Nevada, after we crossed the Arizona border, Lloyd said, "This new freeway opened in December 1973. It cut eight miles off the route between Mesquite and St. George, Utah. The cost was $66 million for this stretch of road, and it took ten years to build. It's one of the most expensive highways in the United States. But it's one of the nicest I've ever seen. Utah Hill used to be dreaded by truck drivers. Especially in the winter. It was dangerous." The highway had been cut through rock cliffs, and again and again it crisscrossed the Virgin River and deep ravines, elevated on pilings.

At Hurricane, Utah, Lloyd pointed to the fertile farms. "People from all over this country come here for peaches, fresh fruits, and corn. We like our produce fresh for canning. Maybe those of you from back East don't put up preserves in Mason jars, but it's still very popular here in the West. People out here like homemade victuals."

Lloyd Smith's descriptions made the entire area come alive in very human terms. His speech wasn't written by somebody else, and it was just right because it wasn't "canned" material. In addition to comments as he drove, Lloyd loaded baggage after each overnight stop, helped people on and off the bus, announced where cabins were located in the parks, advised when meals would be served (and the vouchers that would cover charges). He also gave exact instructions about when the bus would leave for the next destination and exactly where he would pick us up. At the parks, he was available at all hours to answer questions, to introduce people to lodge managers and park rangers, to be helpful.

An eighty-five-year-old woman became ill on the trip. Lloyd arranged for an ambulance to take her to a hospital, kept a check on her progress for other concerned people, and routed the bus to pick her up on the last day. Everyone thanked him for his concern. He was popular with older people, children, everyone in the group.

Lloyd Smith is from Atmore, Alabama, where he took his high school diploma. He was a radio operator in the navy during World War II and drove trucks for Standard Oil of California for ten years before he joined Greyhound as a driver. "Then I was looking for work, and I took a trip on a Greyhound. When I told the driver I could drive big equipment, he told me Greyhound was hiring. I've been with the company ever since. I still make inter-city runs most of the time."

Lloyd Smith's good manners and western informality suit him for his work. He's easygoing and relaxed, and he takes an interest in all his passengers. These are personality traits Greyhound Lines wants.

Job Requirements

Greyhound's regional director of sales development in New York, Frank Korenich, said that "we look for someone who likes people when we're hiring tour escorts. Since our work is seasonal in this region, we hire teachers, educators, nurses, people trained to get along with both individuals and groups. In New York, we get a few actors, and we have Ph.D.'s during school vacations." Work is seasonal, part-time.

Frank Korenich looks for at least two years of college education. Reservations and travel agency experience are also helpful. "People in the trade know the internal workings, the problems encountered on tours, and they know how to meet the problems."

Under general instructions for Greyhound tour escorts, the company gives specific instructions and general advice: "It would be well for all Escorts to adopt the attitude that the passengers are his personal guests, and then they will, we feel certain, provide service consistent with that . . . expected of them by Greyhound," is an introductory statement in the manual.

An escort's conduct is covered as follows: "An Escort should establish himself immediately as the leader-Escort. Give the impression, as courteously as possible but yet firmly, that the prime business affairs of the group are going to be handled his way and not according to the whims of the various members. This can be accomplished most effectively by believing the idea himself. However, DO NOT under pretense of being an authority on an area or a subject be a pseudo-expert." That's a quote; the syntax Greyhound's.

Before new employees are assigned as escorts, they attend a seminar in New York City. That's followed by a seven-day familiarization trip with an experienced guide as instructor. Trainee reactions are reported—"how the trainee acts, how he applies himself to the tour."

There's no age limit for tour escorts. The longest tours from New York are seven days, through New England. In other parts of the country, some tours last for thirty days or more.

Bus Company Addresses
Among the many local and national bus companies, the following are well known:

Gray Line
254 West Fifty-fourth Street
New York, New York 10019

Continental Trailways
315 Continental Avenue
Dallas, Texas 75207

Greyhound Lines
Greyhound Tower
Phoenix, Arizona 85077

Tauck Tours
11 Wilton Road
Westport, Connecticut 06880

RAILROADS

Until they reach management levels, most railroad employees must belong to a union. A seniority system prevails. When a job is available, the opening is posted, and employees may apply for the position; the person who gets the job qualifies by seniority. If two people apply for the opening with similar qualifications, the one with the longer service will be chosen.

The seniority system hampers advancement for those who are fast at learning their work; they must build seniority before they qualify for higher jobs no matter how well prepared they are to make a move to a higher level. But seniority is an advantage for those willing to climb the job ladder at a moderate pace, taking their turn at higher-salaried positions as they come along. Salaries are negotiated by the unions.

From line jobs, senior employees usually move into management. Management at railroads is not under union controls, but some managers maintain union membership as a protection; if their positions are abolished, they may return to line jobs with their seniority intact.

CHIEF DISPATCHER

The dispatcher title has been changed at some railroads, but most employees still use the old title. Although he's supervisor of train operations for Penn Central's Metropolitan Region Operation Control Center, John Cannon is still called chief dispatcher. (Who could remember the newer title?)

John Cannon is in charge of train operations for the Hudson, Harlem, and New Haven divisions in the New York metropolitan area. That involves approximately five hundred commuter trains a day. It's one of the world's largest railroad operations. While great distances are not involved in commuter services, the operations and other characteristics are similar to those at other railroads.

John is in charge of twenty-six dispatchers and several clerks, each assigned to one division. Every dispatcher on the team monitors a territory and is responsible for safe operations along a section of track on a particular branch line. Sophisticated technology serves them in their work. Computers register exact train positions, and dispatchers keep in touch with engineers and on-track crews along the route by telephone. They also can make announcements at stations if there's a delay, or if waiting passengers should be advised to board trains at another track.

During my visit to the Operations Control Center, a fire broke out on a train in Mount Vernon, New York. Tracks had to be closed between Tuckahoe, New York, and the Bronx Botanical Gardens. A signal was sent "to deenergize the tracks," which meant to cut power on the third rails. A fire and maintenance team was dispatched to the location, and passengers at stations were notified by loudspeakers that they should board a train arriving on another track a few minutes later. The assistant manager of station communications, Harry Cunningham, was advised of the fire so callers could be informed about the length of the delay.

Dispatchers started actions immediately after they were alerted to the fire. There was no undue excitement. Each dispatcher knew exactly what to do, and every signal and command was made twice to ensure that there were no further complications. "We double-check and recheck to protect the situation in cases like this," John said.

While these problems were being solved, other trains on the branch line were notified every few minutes about the disabled train, track clearances, and other routines to follow. It was a drama that makes a good story. John and his team worked calmly.

John Cannon has been with the Penn Central System for twenty-eight years. He began as a block operator. You've probably seen signals along railroad tracks. The wide stretches between the signals—sometimes a mile or less, sometimes several miles—are called "blocks." If more than one train is in a particular block, there can be an accident. Block operators keep a constant watch on their blocks, checking signals, keeping in telephone contact with the dispatcher's office, to guarantee smooth, safe operations of trains.

When John Cannon was hired, telegraphy contact was kept with the dispatcher's office, and he'd been trained as a telegrapher in the navy. Eventually John became a freight-handling agent, then he worked in an office. Nowadays he works five days a week, occasionally on weekends when there are special problems. "My hours are 8:00 to 5:00," he said, "but I usually am at the desk by 6:30 A.M."

New Employees

"On the Penn Central, new people coming into this type of work usually start in the towers," John Cannon told me. They work in small buildings—called "towers"—located along the railroad tracks. Some of the buildings aren't towers—they're too low for that—and some are actually in basements. Anyway, the towers are where the railroad's signal networks are located.

The signals are controlled at the towers, and workers in the towers patrol the signals at their locations. Their work is similar to that of block operators.

"It now takes about three years before a person can become a dispatcher," John said. "They have to get used to how trains operate first, and the signal systems. Telegraphy no longer is required because we use radio and telephone and special dispatch lines these days. Dispatch work isn't for everybody. We've had some terrific workers in the towers who've been at a complete loss in dispatch operations. Dispatch work takes an ability to understand the whole system, to handle emergencies, and to keep other things running smoothly."

For assignment to the dispatcher's office, John looks for people who were good tower workers. If they can manage moves, keep trains running on time, and take responsibility for safe operations, they usually become good dispatchers, John believes.

Education is not a key factor in railroad employment. John said that "we have six or seven college graduates in the towers now, but that's not required. Education helps, naturally, but if a person likes railroad work, he or she stays with it. I like it a lot."

Railroad Addresses
Railroad companies have had great financial difficulties during the past several years. As a result, many have merged, and many more have become part of the national railroad system, AMTRAK.

Telephone your local railroad station for information about railroad lines in your area. Or write these following companies:

AMTRAK
955 L'Enfant Plaza S.W.
Washington, D.C. 20024

Penn Central
6 Penn Center Plaza
Room 830
Philadelphia, Pennsylvania 19104

As in New York, local commuter railroad lines have become very important. Many large cities across the country have growing commuter train systems, where rewarding careers offer challenges to many.

TRAVEL MAGAZINES

Years ago some trade journals (magazines and newspapers covering travel industry news, hotels, restaurants, and so forth) had reputations for hiring less qualified personnel than consumer magazines and newspapers. That's no longer true. Nowadays trade journals have some of the best editors and writers. Trade publications are highly competitive. They pay salaries on a par with consumer journals. They require wide experience in interviewing and reporting from new applicants. And they want to see samples of published writing as proof of ability. A college education and wide travel are among pluses for those who apply for work at travel industry trade journals.

For young journalists, trade publications are excellent media for gaining the widest possible exposure to the complex travel and transportation fields. Travel reporters attend press conferences and receptions. They inspect cruise ships. They learn about airplanes, buses, and railroads. They follow legal actions and government regulations. And they cover tourism in the United States and abroad. In short, trade publications are the most fertile ground for learning all about the travel industry.

James C. Glab is an associate editor and staff correspondent at *Travel Agent* magazine. He joined the magazine in November 1972.

Preparing for a career as a journalist, Jim took his bachelor's degree at Columbia University and followed that with a master's degree in journalism at Northwestern University. He specialized in broadcast journalism in school, but the major networks were cutting back on personnel when he graduated. Consequently, he went to work for a suburban newspaper group in Chicago for one and a half years. While in college, he wrote for the *Dubuque Daily.*

At *Travel Agent* magazine, Jim Glab writes news and feature stories, conducts interviews, and attends press conferences. He's traveled on assignments to such diverse places as West Africa, Israel, Europe, Mexico, Central America, and the Caribbean Islands. He's enthusiastic about his work and wants to remain in the travel industry as a writer.

Job Requirements

As the oldest travel industry publication, *Travel Agent* magazine plays an important role. It's read carefully by industry and government officials for its authoritative reports. Eric Friedheim is the magazine's editor and publisher and talked with me about breaking into the field. "Because we cover an interesting worldwide field, we seldom have any problems in finding experienced reporters and editors," he said. When he's hiring editors or reporters, Friedheim looks for maturity first. "We're concerned with how our people act at high-level conferences and how well they can write hard-core news stories."

News breaks fast in the travel industry—and that's another guideline to the types of people who can handle editorial or writing assignments for industry trade publications. They must be able to write both feature and news stories quickly. Usually work on a daily newspaper is the best training for such stiff journalistic demands.

TRAVEL
WRITER

Travel writers write travel guide books and magazine and news-paper articles. Several have become radio and television personalities. Their field is travel—where to go, what to see, what to do as a traveler.

Travel writers spend a great deal of time away from home—sometimes seven to eight months each year. That's somewhat disruptive on the home scene, constantly separating writers from their families and their friends. Living out of a suitcase can be fatiguing, and constant travel requires stamina. Adjusting to changing climatic conditions (from frigid cold to tropical heat or vice versa) in a few hours is difficult for some people. It's not all a bowl of cherries, as the old song says. But for those who like it, few professions are more exciting than travel writing.

Gay Nagle Myers is a travel writer and editor with East/West Network in New York City. East/West publishes magazines for such companies as United, Allegheny, and Delta airlines, and for Holiday Inns. Their combined readership numbers in the millions every month.

Gay attended the University of Texas in Austin and was graduated with a degree in journalism. She'd lived in New York City when she was young and wanted to return "to the Big Apple," as she puts it. During her senior year in college, she went to New York for interviews.

"At *The New York Times,* I was told to return to Texas and work for five years, then to reapply for a reporting or feature writing job," she said. "Interviews were discouraging, to say the least. Then McGraw-Hill Publishing sent out a notice that they were setting up a college graduate editorial training program. They accepted seven girls from across the country, and I was one of the seven. That September I entered the program." But Gay thought it was more secretarial training than editorial preparation, so she quit and went to Europe, where she traveled widely. When she returned, an employment agency sent her to a trade publication. She was hired as an assistant editor at a low salary. In a few months, she became an associate editor, then editorial director of *Interline Reporter,* a magazine for airline employees. She remained with the trade press for six years.

"With that experience," Gay explained, "I felt qualified to take on more responsibility. And I began to search for a creative outlet in the field, one that would reach a wide consumer public rather than just travel industry people. I found it at East/West." As New York editor for the publishing company, Gay writes about travel. But she's branched out into entertainment, home furnishings, and other topics. "It's an expansive outlet for me, and challenging. I learn something new every day," she said. "And I really love it."

In her work at trade publications and at East/West, Gay Nagle Myers has traveled throughout the world. She's been to every continent except Antarctica—and that could be her next assignment.

"Travel is a wonderful field for a journalist," Gay believes. "But you have to *like* it. It's not for everyone, not for the homebody who regrets every moment spent away from his or her family, not for the types who shudder at meeting new people everywhere on every trip. When they're away a lot, some people feel that they're shirking their responsibilities as parents. They probably are. Adjustments must be made.

"I think that a distinctive personality type enjoys travel writing. Of course, an ability to write organized news and feature stories is most important. But a deeper interest in the things that make travel fascinating also is part of the individual's personal makeup. Art and architecture, history, languages, furniture design, sports, cooking (French, Chinese, German, other cuisines), wildlife, sociology, political problems, the ethnic traditions that make people different from country to country—they're intermingled in this work."

You can't separate these wide interests from the things that a travel writer must explore to refine this craft. In inspecting a hotel or a cruise ship, contemporary design, antiques, other elements must be assessed. Are towels thick and absorbent, for instance. Is the plumbing good? Are closets big enough? Is service in dining rooms pleasant, and how is the food? Can travelers buy film at the newsstand? Are prices competitive? Is the atmosphere informal or dressy? Is the hotel deluxe, as the advertising says, or should it be designated as first class or in a lower category? Can people walk safely in the neighborhood, and is it near other tourist attractions?

These are the practical things, which must be balanced by "good taste," a phrase that's gone out of style. Nonetheless, the best travel writers are critics, looking for the proper balances in quality and service. If places are unappealing, and people aren't getting their money's worth, it's up to travel writers to say so. Their advice to readers is important.

As a travel writer, Gay Nagle Myers has served her apprenticeship. Wide travel is an absolute necessity; Gay got that on her own and in her work with the trade publications. She enjoys reading and keeps current on the latest trends, new resorts, new areas of interest. Whether she's on a photo safari, in a Paris restaurant, at an Alpine ski resort, or in Hong Kong, she judges what she sees. The appeals—and the things that detract from rewarding travel—are her milieu. That's what travel writing is all about.

These multi-phased interests apply to all travel writing—

travel guide books, feature articles, newspaper and magazine columns, broadcast material. Within the restrictions of an individual writing style, every professional travel writer looks into more than just going someplace.

Job Requirements
Courses in journalism have become increasingly important as preparation for travel writing. However, many writers prepared themselves as English and literature majors in college. Most also worked on school newspapers and magazines, which is invaluable experience. A working knowledge of one or more foreign languages is helpful but not absolutely necessary.

Before most writers move into travel writing, they've held jobs as editors, reporters, or feature writers with newspapers and magazines. They know how to interview people, how to approach investigative reporting, the journalistic basics.

Wide travel also is a must, but that sometimes can come on the job, on assignments with some publications.

**FREE-LANCE
TRAVEL WRITING**

Many writers yearn to get into the free-lance field, to be self-employed. That's true among travel writers as well. Without contractual commitments, and an assured income, however, free-lance travel writing can be difficult. Only a few professional free-lance travel writers have managed to make a good living. It can be a deceptive and frustrating dream. The experts who know the world and whose names are known by editors get first consideration. Rightfully, because they've proved themselves, and their work is known to be dependable.

Anyone who has not been published widely, and who has not developed associations with tourist offices, airlines, ship lines, the entire travel industry, will have great difficulties trying to compete as a free-lance travel writer.

FOREIGN TOURIST OFFICE

Several foreign countries have established tourist offices in the United States. Their purpose is to promote tourism to their countries, to distribute information to the traveling public, and to serve as liaison between their government offices and the working press.

Because the American northeast is the primary market for foreign tourism, New York City offices are the biggest and have the largest staffs. New York is where foreign governments are most likely to hire Americans.

Important public relations posts at tourist offices are usually held by Americans. There are several reasons for this. Recognition among editors, journalists, television and radio representatives is an asset, and few foreigners have established such relationships. Public relations in this country also requires facility in writing and speaking English.

Those in charge must know how and where to place news releases and press kits, and how and where to channel information to media outlets. They must write speeches, run press conferences, stage presentations, and supervise detailed arrangements for receptions and social gatherings. Professional experience is an absolute necessity.

With few exceptions, public relations directors with foreign tourist offices have had their writing published widely. Most speak foreign languages. And most have worked closely with tourism abroad. Several years' experience, an ability to deal with foreign officials on ambassadorial and ministerial levels and to manage a staff (sometimes spread across the country in branch offices) are among the requirements.

Obviously, young people just entering the job market are unqualified to step into these top-salaried positions. With experience and the proper qualifications, though, handling public relations for a foreign government is a respected profession.

George L. Hern, Jr., public relations director at the French Government Tourist Office in New York, is a professional who has earned a listing in *Who's Who.* He was graduated from the University of California with a B.A. in French, following that with a year's graduate work in education and studies for two years at the Sorbonne in Paris. (He was a classroom instructor while in college.) After completing his studies, he worked for the U.S. State Department in France for two years.

In 1954 George joined the personnel department at Air France in New York. Within less than a year, he transferred to the airline's public relations department, where he worked for eleven years. He followed that with six years as a reporter and feature story writer for a Florida-based newspaper chain and magazines. When the French government was searching for a public relations director in 1972, he was invited to apply for the job and was hired. George speaks French and knows France as well as (or better than) most French people.

Public relations for foreign countries has been described by some as "a multi-headed monster." Without a doubt, it requires good organization. Since American business methods and promotional techniques are different from those in other nations, the person in charge must balance the work flow within two national frameworks. Furthermore, government bureaucracy works at a pace different from commercial operations, requiring more paper work, reports to government headquarter offices, requests for authorization of plans months in advance, and budgetary applications to cover office management for a year or more.

A public relations director for a foreign government, in short, runs a business office with government backing. While he (or she) is responsible for conducting the business of public relations effectively, he must deal tactfully with appointed officials and offices with entirely different outlooks and approaches. Public relations representatives for foreign tourist offices, as a well-known journalist saw it, are "diplomats with typewriters, and a sense of humor."

On a daily schedule, George Hern writes press releases and provides information to media representatives. He produces scripts for television and ghostwrites speeches for French government officials. He conducts seminars for travel agents and the press. He gives lectures, supervises exhibits at trade shows, organizes and conducts press trips to France. He takes charge of film and photograph distribution, and he serves as liaison between the advertising agency and tourist office management. He also checks travel guide books on France for accuracy. It's demanding work, but interesting.

"I also work, occasionally, in a quasi-official capacity, with French wine and food distributors," George Hern said, "and with French railroads and public information people at the French Embassy." These activities are seldom spelled out as specific duties for public relations representatives, but they coexist as diplomatic necessities in most foreign-government tourist offices.

Responsibilities in this job category may have unusual twists: as former public relations director for the Spanish Ministry of Information and Tourism in North America, I handled similar nonofficial extras. Among them, I was responsible for the annual Spanish Day Parade on New York's Fifth Avenue— with floats, marching bands, a gala formal ball, and public events staged for a week each year. I arranged gallery showings throughout the country for Spanish artists and tours for folkloric dance and music groups sent from Spain. Probably the most surprising assignment was to provide a dozen horse-drawn antique Spanish carriages (with drivers and Spanish stallions) for the opening of the Indianapolis 500. And during Hemisfair in San Antonio, Texas, where the Spanish government built a pavilion and installed $60 million in art works from the Prado Museum in Madrid, I hired people to work on the staff, arranged for flamenco dance groups as entertainers, and supervised the publicity. During my years as a Spanish government employee, the work never was dull.

Job Requirements

"Writing and speaking abilities are important in this type of job," George Hern advises. "It adds up to a public relations personality, an ability to think and speak on your feet." He also believes that a public relations representative for a foreign country must have enthusiasm, that it helps to know about music, art, architecture, and geography and to have a broad range of interests.

If you want to be in public relations for a foreign government, you should seek such work only after you've gained experience. That means previous work in public relations, published writing, speaking before groups, and managing a staff in other jobs. It also means facility in a foreign language, international training, and a fair amount of tact and patience.

Americans working for foreign tourist offices hold a unique standing in the travel industry. They're respected in the United States and in the nations they represent. And as I said before, the work is never dull.

CRUISE STAFF

"Cruise ships really are resort hotels at sea," stated Lee Vanderburg, coordinator of entertainment for the Marine Hotel Department at Holland America Cruises. "Our needs are similar to those of hotels, and that applies to food and beverage management, hostesses, and staff. Our cruise staff people are American."

Most cruise staff employees begin as part-time or summer help. At Holland America, Mr. Vanderburg looks "for young men, who are willing to run a lot." They handle stage setups, lighting, and microphones. They're assigned to instruct in deck sports, swimming, and Ping-Pong, to run quiz shows and group games. They may serve as masters of ceremonies in lounges at night, introducing entertainers. After a season or two—or as they become well seasoned in the work—they may be promoted to assistant cruise director jobs.

For cruise staffs, interviewers look for college students with pleasant personalities, individuals "who are good with people." A well-groomed appearance is mandatory. While I was at Holland America Cruises waiting to meet those who do the hiring for cruise ships, a young woman arrived to apply for a job. She was qualified to work aboard a cruise ship as an arts and crafts teacher, she had worked with both adults and children in groups, and she appeared to be self-assured. I heard later that she didn't get the job, but I wasn't surprised.

The young woman arrived at the office wearing blue jeans, sneakers, and a sloppy ski jacket. Since the young woman apparently was unaware that she was improperly attired for a job interview, it's unfortunate that someone had not advised her. A businesslike appearance is important for anyone applying for a job; the individual entering an office in the garb described seldom gets hired. "Did you ever see anyone applying for a job in a getup like that?" asked another man in the waiting room. "I think she's already lost the job."

"Because we have many older people on our cruises, the people we hire must be patient and understanding," said Mr. Vanderburg. "Previous work in summer camps or teaching crafts is helpful background for supervising children's programs on the ships. Another asset to hiring is musical talent." When applicants can play musical instruments, or if they have good voices, they can work with entertainers. "We can always use lounge pianists and guitarists. Even an ability to do magic tricks can be useful."

Hostesses aboard ships are generally chosen from mature women aged thirty-five to fifty. Young women are seldom hired for this work. Holland America Cruises looks for patient and helpful women, not too glamorous, who cater to passengers' well-being. They must have the good manners to socialize easily. And being able to wear evening clothes and resort wear stylishly is important.

Cruise ship hostesses are expected to make passengers feel welcome, to see that they enjoy themselves. Their title tells the story; they're hostesses, as they would be with guests in their homes. Often retired airline stewardesses become cruise hostesses. Their training with people and the personalities best suited for such work are similar.

Pay for cruise staffs is "modest," but all food, lodging, and travel are provided. Staff members often supplement their salaries by working as photographers or dance instructors, and teaching golf at ports of call. For such supplemental extras, tips usually are generous.

Job Requirements

Arts and crafts teachers are sought for cruises during school vacation periods. Those who can teach "on a comparatively simple level" fill the need. A person who can teach needlepoint is an example, or one who can instruct in jewelry design. Crafts requiring complicated equipment aren't taught aboard ships.

The sports-minded individual who can teach swimming, deck tennis, and other shipboard sports has an advantage. Those good at golf and tennis may be assigned as instructors or partners at ports of call. With the exception of youth counselors, which are summer jobs primarily, ship lines hire cruise staff personnel throughout the year.

And those who play guitar, piano, or sing may qualify for part-time employment.

Ship Line Addresses

Although the United States Line and several other major ship lines in the United States have ceased passenger services, several foreign companies based in the United States (or with American branches) continue to serve American ports.

American Canadian Line
461 Water Street
P.O. Box 368
Warren, Rhode Island 02885

Chandris Cruises
666 Fifth Avenue
New York, New York 10019

Holland America Cruises
2 Penn Plaza
New York, New York 10001

Norwegian Caribbean Lines
100 Biscayne Boulevard
Miami, Florida 33132

Princess Cruises
3435 Wilshire Boulevard
Los Angeles, California 90010

Royal Viking Line
1 Embarcadero Center
San Francisco,
   California 94111

SHIP LINE PUBLIC RELATIONS

As with foreign tourist offices and airlines, foreign-owned ship lines offer excellent public relations opportunities for Americans.

Again, experienced professionals—who can write news releases and have a good record in getting print-media and broadcast coverage—hold the important jobs. Most have a news or magazine editorial and writing background. But some have been promoted to top positions after working in the department for some years. However they may have risen to the directorial jobs, they've learned public relations techniques, the responsiblities and day-to-day routines that effective work demands.

From Tulsa, Oklahoma, Oscar F. Kolb is public relations director at Holland America Cruises. It's a Dutch company incorporated in the United States.

Oscar Kolb was graduated from the University of Tulsa with a B.A. in journalism. While still in college, he worked as a radio announcer and newsman and also handled television promotion assignments. He continued in these capacities directly after college.

Then he was hired by the Shell Oil Corporation in Tulsa, where he was an editor and writer for company publications. He also handled some public relations assignments. Eventually he transferred to Houston, then to New York City. During his five years with Shell, Oscar worked mainly on corporate regional publications. In 1962 he joined Holland America Cruises and has headed their public relations department ever since.

Oscar Kolb distributes press releases to consumer and trade media. He places "blurbs" (short paragraphs) about passengers in society columns. On cruises, he's in charge of press groups. And he stages receptions for travel agents and journalists when ships are in port. Dinner, dancing, and entertainment are among amenities at receptions, but information kits about the ships, speeches, and sales presentations are also integrated into the format. Oscar is responsible for the material distributed, for seeing that invitations are sent to people who will help increase sales or otherwise promote Holland America Cruises. He often writes speeches for ship line executives to be delivered at the receptions.

"Our efforts are directed to keeping the company's name in the public eye," Oscar declared. "That means getting publicity for our sailing schedules, for our cruises, and for the ports we visit." On two occasions, he has been the company executive in charge of tours to China, which required arranging visas (not an easy accomplishment in China), lecturing, and briefing passengers about what to expect.

Oscar's many duties don't stop there. He writes regularly for twenty-five newspapers and trade publications. He supervises filming and production of promotional films, and writes and has brochures printed for each cruise. And he makes certain that the photographic library is up to date for use by editors and writers.

Job Requirements
"For the working ship line public relations person," Oscar Kolb says, "a journalism degree is the best background. Anyone

who has to deal with so many journalists does best if he understands their needs and work demands. The background eases contact with others in the field. I was editor of our college newspaper; that was invaluable to me later, when I went into full-time work. My radio and TV work also were helpful."

Oscar believes that an outgoing personality is a must. "You can't be a mouse and get results in this field."

Travel benefits are among sideline attractions for employees at Holland America Cruises. After a year's employment, all people with the company "from the mailroom up" may go on cruises at 25 percent of minimum cost. "That's a very nice benefit," Oscar said.

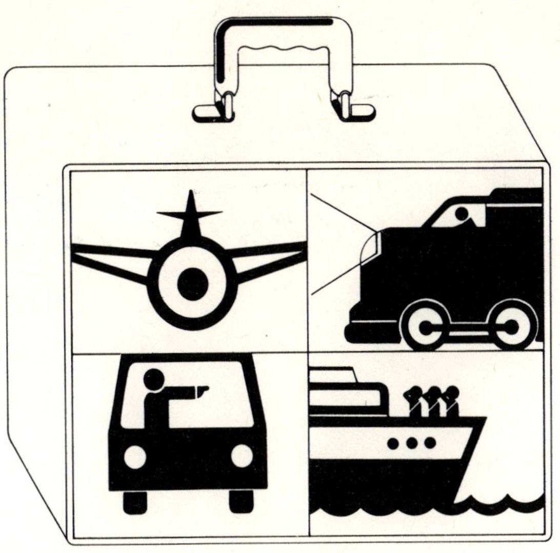

A SUMMING UP

The entire world—dazzling cities, small towns and villages, remote deserts and steaming jungles—is open to people who have chosen to follow travel careers.

Many women and men have worked their way to the highest executive ranks in the travel industry. You don't have to begin in an important job to reach the top, either. One well-known airline president started as a baggage handler at a small Texas airport. A travel editor on a national magazine took her first trip to Europe on a discount, when she was an airline reservations agent. Now she travels around the world as an editor with all expenses paid. And a former bus tour guide recently became sales manager for an international hotel chain. These stories are far from unusual.

So if you should decide to work in the vast and varied travel industry, think about the many jobs described in this book. Any one of them could be a step toward a rewarding lifetime career.

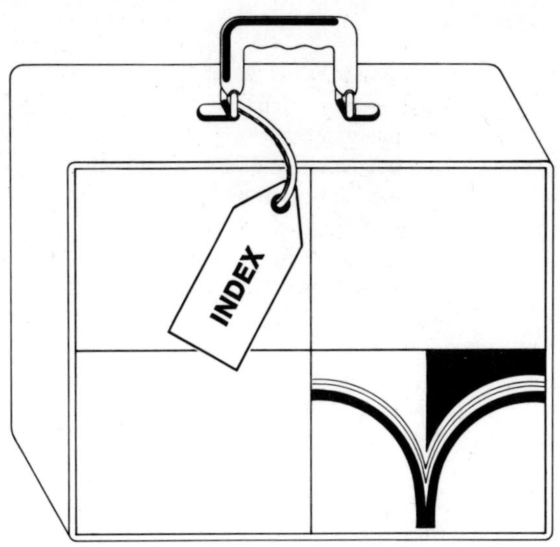
INDEX

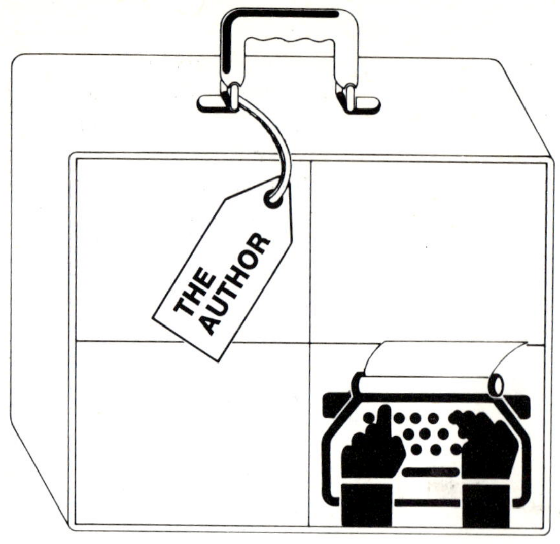

Ralph H. Peck has been to places most of us only dream of visiting. The more than two thousand articles he has written about faraway places have appeared in the New York *Daily News,* the Boston *Globe,* the *Cleveland Magazine, Town and Country, Holiday,* and other periodicals and newspapers. He is the author of twenty books—among them, *Getaway Guides, $10-a-Day Guides,* and *Young City Guides* to help travelers make the most of their leisure time. In his travels, Peck has interviewed Amazon headhunters, the Pope, film stars, kings, and Olympic athletes. But, most of all, he has talked with men and women who work in the travel business. He is uniquely qualified to give an insider's view of their lives and work.